Osmund Airy

**Letters Addressed to the Earl of Lauderdale**

Osmund Airy

**Letters Addressed to the Earl of Lauderdale**

ISBN/EAN: 9783337109226

Printed in Europe, USA, Canada, Australia, Japan

Cover: Foto ©ninafisch / pixelio.de

More available books at **www.hansebooks.com**

# LETTERS

ADDRESSED TO THE

# EARL OF LAUDERDALE.

---

## EDITED BY OSMUND AIRY.

---

PRINTED FOR THE CAMDEN SOCIETY.

M.DCCC.LXXXIII.

# PREFACE.

The Editor hopes in a future volume of the Society's publications to offer a selection from the correspondence comprised in the Lauderdale Papers. That selection will be framed with the view of illustrating with some fulness the main stream of the political history of Scotland during the reign of Chàrles II., or, rather, during the supremacy of Lauderdale in Scotch affairs. The letters now printed have been taken out of that correspondence as being, to a great extent, isolated in their interest, while in themselves curious. The first eleven are written by John Kennedy, Earl of Cassilis, father of Lady Margaret Kennedy, with whom Lauderdale entertained so close an intimacy, and who afterwards became the wife of Gilbert Burnet.

"Don John," as he is familiarly called by Tweeddale and others, was one of the most marked figures in Scotland at the beginning of the reign. He was noted, and is continually referred to in the Lauderdale correspondence, as a proud, obstinate old man, dressed in strange fashion, and eccentric in language and opinions. His eccentricity was perhaps most to be noted in the sturdy integrity with which, alone among the politicians who surrounded him, he refused for fear or favour to betray his rigid Presbyterian principles, by taking the oath of allegiance, which in his eyes implied the royal supremacy in ecclesiastical affairs. He died in April 1668. Any-one who reads the letters of Lady Margaret Kennedy, published by

the Bannatyne Club, will be struck by the similarity between father
and daughter in style and tone alike.

The remaining thirty-three letters are from two of the most
distinguished of those numerous soldiers of fortune who left
Scotland to command the regiments of Scotch guards always
maintained by the French sovereign. Those from Lord Rutherford, afterwards Earl Teviot, give a vivid picture of the harass-
ments attending the command of an outstanding garrison, as well
as many curious scraps of information. It is interesting too to
notice in them that the wild and varied life in foreign countries
seemed never to weaken the strength of the national feeling.
Rutherford is always a Scotchman in the first place, and we are
vividly reminded of the picture which Scott drew of his class
in the character of Lord Crawford in " Quentin Durward." He
was killed in or about the year 1665, in a skirmish with the Moors at
Tangiers, of which he was made governor after the sale of Dunkirk.

The letters from Lord George Douglas illustrate the complications which necessarily arose between the French government and
these mercenary troops, when disagreements occurred between the
two crowns; and they as well as Lord Rutherford's form an interesting addition to the information given us by Mr. Burton, in " The
Scot abroad," and M. Michel in " Les Ecossais en France." The
papers are taken from the Additional MSS. in the British Museum.

The Editor reserves for a future occasion the pleasure of acknow-
ledging the assistance so courteously rendered to him at the MSS.
Department of the British Museum, while engaged upon the
Lauderdale correspondence.

# LETTERS ADDRESSED

TO THE

# EARL OF LAUDERDALE.

### EARL OF CASSILIS TO THE EARL OF LAUDERDALE.

MY LORD,                    Edinb. 28 deʳ, 1660.      23114, f. 111.

I waited for yours with anxietis and reseaved it with muche satisfaction, returning your Loᴾ now manie heartie thankes for your respect to my cousin, tho for hazard of the monosillabes reputation I wishe it had onely come two dayes sooner. Your Lo. may give assurance that whatsoever my thoghts wer long since for kingly autoritie I am not come so farre to anie extremitie as to forget my dutie to our native prince, or prove ingrate for his Mˢ kindness to Scotland. Bot my earnest desire is that hee may so regulate his power that the lustre of his government may keep his subjects with delight under him and prove ane attractive to strangers, who (as all men) love to embrace there apprehendit happines. If anie should enquire why the king's plantations are so farre scattered, since by vicinitis they may bee the more help full to eache other, and with lesse trouble to the croũne, I wold know what to answer. It is thoght the Spanishe monarchie is the lesse formidable by the great disfraction of her limbes. Whatsoever bee undertaken by these dominions, that the blessing may be expected, let it bee on cleer grounds. Jamaica gives mee some occasion of this. I doubt not bot your stay there may bee of great use, yet it vexes me to thinke with whom I shall communicate and advise the following one the project that is not yet communicable,[a] and which untimeously vented may bee marred. The instructions your Lo. mentiones please mee well and conduce to the end.    If you shall procure ane addition by letter in serious termes to the commissioner for laying to heart and promoving what shall bee propond by your incatenato[b] for inlarging his Majesties dominions and multipliing his subjects, it may doe well being timely delivered by mee.    If you bee instrumentall to increase our king's greatnes in a Christian and heroik way I hope a greater then man will give the reward like himselfe, that you may doe and get that from his free grace is the cordiall wishe of

Your mere incatenato.

---

### EARL OF CASSILIS TO THE EARL OF LAUDERDALE.

23115, f. 4.    MY LORD,                                        Edenb. 1 Ja. 1661.
Since my writing the other, beside my differing from the rest in parl[iament] for choosing our preesident, I differd upon the oathe preposid,[c] and whatsoever there determination bee, except I see a a more cleer ground for it then I judge possible to shou, ere I take it, I resolve to leave his Majesties counsels and dominions, whiche

---

[a] The  project mentioned in this and succeeding letters is probably the confirmation of the Presbyterian government, which Lauderdale urged upon Charles as being the best way to secure Scotland in his interest in case of complications with his English subjects.  Burnet mentions a long letter written to Cassilis' daughter, Margaret Kennedy, by Lauderdale on this subject.  *See*, on the whole matter, *Burnet*, vol. i. sect. 108.

[b] Italian " incatenare," to bind.

[c] The oath of allegiance which acknowledged the King's supremacy in ecclesiastical matters.  *See* Mackenzie's *Memoirs*, p. 23.

He was declared incapable of trust on April 10, after a second refusal, when summoned as an extraordinary lord of session.  *See* 23116, ff. 17, 19.

is as ill as anie thing that ever Oliver threatned mee with, tho he knew I abhorid him and his way. If I sit and can bee of anie use for promoving that project whiche you onely knou, it will bee expedient letters bee written seriously to such as bear suey besides the commissioner which was shewed to your Lo. at my being there by

Your *incatenato*.

I pray your Lo. let mee not long so muche for the answer of this as of my former.

If his Majestie thinke I merite anie trust I hope hee will intrust the letters and timeing of the deliverie to mee, and let mee kenn somewhat of the tenoŭr.

---

EARL OF CASSILIS TO THE EARL OF LAUDERDALE.

MY LORD,                    Edenb. 8 Ja. 1661.    23115, f. 8.

Since your stay is necessitat, if I by our parlaments command bee made incapable to acte in that bussines whiche I communicate to you onely, I hope his Majesties justice will not put mee to worke when my hands are cut off. The causes of there proced . . . I have set doune in a paper aparte under a more legible hand. If I had leav to prosecute that project, the helpe of the monosillabe of whom I wrote lately to you might have beene of great use; he is nou to his home in the countrey, upon his disabling to sit here as a member, and that (as I suspect) by the cumming and his fliing of one against whom you formerly at Striveling* protected him. Tho you onely knou the whole, yet I glanced at severall things conducing to it with him long since, which makes me knoŭ, hee wald

* Stirling.

sympathize and assist powerfully by his pen when a doore opens if hee bee not put in a capacitie to acte otherwise. I have made bold to write a line to his Majestie, and if there bee need I hope you will helpe to read it to him, and imparte more at large upon conveniencie what I have written to you. I shall trouble your Lo. no more now bot to shew that your returne will bee longed for by

Your *incatenato.*

### EARL OF CASSILIS TO CHARLES II.

23115, f. 10.  MAY IT PLEASE YOUR MAJESTIE,

Whil upon your command I was here attending your Majesties service in parlament ane oathe was urged whiche I desired to bee explaind that I might take it with freedome, and tho they without contradiction . . . . agreed, that what I propond was there true meaning, yet they refused to adde it in write. If upon this I bee secluded from a capacitie to prosecute, as I intendit that project which I imparted to your Majestie, and by your command more at large to another (whom you and manie of your subjects confide in), I hope your Majestie will not blame mee to sit idle when I am disabled to worke, and till I deserve worse must presume you will esteeme mee that whiche I resolve to live and die,

Your Majesties faithfull and humble subject,

CASSILLIS.

Edenb. 8 Ja. 1661.

## EARL OF CASSILIS TO THE EARL OF LAUDERDALE.

MY LORD,                                                    23115, f. 100.

It might appear to some you had missed the copie of my reasons inclosed in one of my last to you, for you nether ansuer nor mention them, and I thoght you kneu mee too well to send mee offers instead of ansuers, bot I hope wee shall not bee hastie to mistake. As to the places which his Majestie pleases to nominat mee for,[a] you knou I am free from moving for them, and if the barres that ly in the way bee taken out I shall endeavour to serve him faithfully in them, if my former cariage deserve not so muche as the removeall of these. I should be sorrie that his Majestie should wrong himself, the people, and you, whom I take mee to as the remembrancer at least, to nominat suche a one. Wee have not manie newes here. It is said they are going on with the processes, and that contest about the acte craved to bee past betuixt creditor and debitor is like to make heat, manie being interest on bothe sides. What is more to bee exprest looke in another paper hirewith under a sure hand from

Edenb. 7 Mar. 1661[?].

                                    Your incatenato.

---

## EARL OF CASSILIS TO THE EARL OF LAUDERDALE.

MY LORD,                                                    23116, f. 15.

I hope you will beleeve I am sensible of his Majesties favours, and my gratitude for them obliges to keep my selfe free of that staine of ambition by suallowing doune nou the pilles I have so long stucke at, as may make me unserviceable to him, in that designe whiche I conceave may be of consequence for him.

---

[a] Cassilis was nominated a member of the Scotch Privy Council, 1661, Feb. 13.

Whether for that upon the proofes his Majestie hes alreadie had of my fidelitie he will please to dispense with neu tyes it belongs to himselfe to consider. What more I had to say is set doune otherwise, being unwilling you should receave unnecessar trouble by

Your incatenato.

Edenb. 6 Apr. 1661.

ᵃWhether your friends saying his Majestie was at Whitehall and his commissioner here merites the castle threatned and confinement to the toune execute you may enquire at conveniencie.

More of this if not nou with the next.

---

## EARL OF CASSILIS TO THE EARL OF LAUDERDALE.

23116, f. 17.                                            Apryle 6, 1661.

The Notte to which the letter of your incatenato relates.

What past anent the oath in the beginning of the parliament is showen; and now the Earle of Cassilis being required to come to the parliament as one nominat to be an extraordinar on the sessione he appeared (tho he had a promeise before from the Commissioner his grace of a post warrand to waite on his Majestie), and being required to give his oath and subscrybe a declaratione which wes large and never formerlie seene be him, he acknowledged he had seene the oath long since, bot the declaration being new and large he desyred tyme to consider. Withall declared he wes willing to serve his Majestie in whatsoever statione he wes capable of, bot for shunning misconstructione of his ansuer desired there allowance to waite upon his Majestie. The Chancellerᵇ in passione and heate ansuered: " The King's power and authoritie is heire." The Earle ansuered, " That is not denyed, bot yet the King is at Whythall."

ᵃ *See* following letter.                              ᵇ Glencairn.

Then the Chancellez said, "You dissoune the King's Commissioner," which the said Earle contradicted, bot wes still interrupted
in passione and removed, and reinformed by eare witness that it wes
moved by some to send the Earle to the castell, and the result wes
that he should appeare and give his ansüer on Tüisday the 9th, and
remaine confyned in Edinburgh in the meane tyme.
What the designe wes to hinder him from going up is best
knowen to the actors.

---

### EARL OF CASSILIS TO THE EARL OF LAUDERDALE.

MY LORD,                                                        23116, f. 19.
　　If I have not merited the libertie to wait upon his Majestie for
representing my reasons in reference to my cariage upon the oathe
and declaration of parlament, when I conceave it for some advanc-
ment of his oune service, I shall regrate it and studie to deserve
better in whatsoever condition I bee under his Majestie. I have
writ so muche to your Lo. on this subject as I shall spair further till
to-morrou ordaind for a finall ansuer to bee given by [a]
　　　　　　　　　　　　　　　　　　　　　Your incatenato.
Edenb. 9 Apr. 1661.

---

### EARL OF CASSILIS TO THE EARL OF LAUDERDALE.

MY LORD,                          East Roxburghe, 28 7ber [1667].    23128, f. 74.
　　I have muche satisfaction by yours of the 20th, and heartily wishe
a progresse sutable to the actings mentiond in it. I intind not to

---

[a] *See* footnote, p. 2.

make evill use of it, in reference to him most concerned.[a]  The
going on that way is thoght a surer mean for quieting spirites then
raising of oppressing men under whatsoever name.   I shall be brief
henc, purposing by a surer bearer tho slouer, that you shall have the
trouble of some lines more from

Your incatenato.

### EARL OF CASSILIS TO THE EARL OF LAUDERDALE.

MY LORD,                          East Roxburghe, 30 7ber [1667].

It appeares by yours of the 20th that Donald[b] hes fallen on a
handsome way to discharge himselfe,[c] and the going on at that rate
you write,[d] a probable mean to the ends whiche honest men desire
bee aimed at.   It will not bee secure nor noble to doe his worke by
halfes.   His keeping stedfast friendship with those of our profession
beyond sea[e] is a goode meane for making him indeed Donald on
that element, probably likewise in plantations, and for breaking the
bridge[f] whiche his great neighbour might have troubled us by.
It is no shame to imitate a woman (who ruled famously) in the
support of the protestant cause bot glorious to outgoe her.   I wishe
hee had a true convert in his bosome,[g] I am sure it is a dutie to use
the meanes, and I can imagine nothing obliging to a tolleration of

---

[a] Probably referring to Earl Rothes, the King's Commissioner, who at this time had
his commission taken away.  In a letter to Lauderdale, dated Sept. 7, 1667, Tweeddale says: " For God's sake, let us but have a trial of securing the peace and quiet
of the country without a commissioner, having a chancellor and the old form of
government."
[b] Charles II.                          [e] From the war with the Dutch.
[d] Probably the negociations which ended in the Triple Alliance.
[e] Holland.                          [f] French conquest of Holland [?].
[g] The Duke of York [?]

superstition and idolatrie. The actings of those in his station are exemplari. I need not repeat to you the poets sentence to that purpose. If it bee a goode worke to gain one soule what must it bee to bring in millions running headlong in the broad way, either plainly worshipping divils, or at best ther oune fancies without neglecting our oune ignorants at home. Hou well might a parte of that wasted in the 3 kingdomes on belligods bee bestowed for præserving worlds of heathen. If parents providing temporall things for there children bee a great addition to the naturall obligation, hou muche should providing spirituall and faithfull steuarts to distribute ingage the hearts of suche as doe or shall beeleeve (on right grounds) ane immortalitie. I have sent abroad a youth on whom paines have beene tane for advancing him in knouledge, perhaps not without successe, some advise it for lousing his tongue and making what hee hes more communicative. My designe is that hee may bee made more serviceable to our almightie king and his vicegerent and generally to all to whom hee oues dutie. I hope you will not bee spairing of advice to him and so comme another incatenato, and likewise to Mr. Pat. Lyon, who hes attendit him these five years past you may use freedome with him, for hee will bee found muche above the pitche of those who take them to suche employment. I wishe they may be hasted away when the youth hes done his dutie to his Majestie and the rest of the royall familie as you will direct. I hope you will please to signifie your minde in reference to a students cariage to the Prince of Orange and others there at his comming or afterwards, I thinke hee will not have occasion to fall in that ceremoniall solæcisme which Hemfleet in haste made a friend commit. This occasion makes mee præsume to bee the more large, whiche I trust you will not mistake in

Your incatenato.

If you shall procure from his Majestie suche allowance for going abroad or recommendation as hes been given to others of his condition, it will bee a further obligation.

## Earl of Cassilis to the Earl of Lauderdale.

23128, f. 85.

My Lord, East Roxburghe, 1 Oct. [1667].

Since the writing of my other of yesterdayes date I have thoght of some things which the bearer, Henry Kennedy, can informe and concern his Majestie to knou. He is so well knoune to you and others employed as you wer, as it seemes needles to write how faithfully he did acquit himself in everie station hee was set in, and how well hee deserves trust. Hee is to speake of some particulars whereof you have heard (as I thinke) muche alreadie. I hope you will make your best use of what hes speaks. If anie of his relations have beene wrongd, or himselfe frustrat of what is due to him, your help will yet further oblige,

Your incatenato.

---

## Lord Rutherford to the Earl of Lauderdale.

23116, f. 2.

My Lord, [30 March, 1661.]

Displease your Lo. I must, since little better as stealing I ame casting your l: moneys at the cocks. Your two sutes of cloaths are bocht with the consent of three different enouch fancies other wayes of taylours and courtiers, all the other things contained in the memoire are also bespoken so yt your Lo. sall hav them w$^t$ in the tyme prefixed. Your 200$^{lb}$ ster. will pairt fro your Lo. thoe to Mr. Kinlochs great grudging, soit dit entre nous, I did buy all myself, he looking on w$^t$ ready moneys, which saved allwayes 5 of the hindred.

At my arryval heir Mr. Le Tellier,[a] secretaire of State, caressed

---

[a] Noted for his persecution of the Huguenots. His last signature was given to the Revocation of the Edict of Nantes. *See* Felice, *Histoire des Protestants de France*, pp. 399, 411.

me much, prodigalising the King's favors on me, and did propose to
keep our reg<sup>t</sup> at 20 companies, making them to 2000 sogers, but be
the reduction of Lo. George Douglas reg<sup>t</sup> into ours, but when we
came to conclude our traitte he told me I behoved to renonce the
title and qualitie of Scots Gardes. This did so move me yt I
replyed (in good earnest) yt not only would I loose all my preten-
sions and fortune, yea, but rather suffer the rake befor I con-
discended to so base ane agreement. The regiment belonged to the
nation not to me, and y<sup>t</sup> no man heirafter could w<sup>t</sup> assurance treat
w<sup>t</sup> the King of France since he would violat his bargaines made so
authentiquely and signed be his secretaires of State. He seing me
so hotanosed, left me to myself, and I went immediatly to my Lo.
St. Albans and related what had passed. The Duk of Anious
fiancailles are to be this day, to-morrow the marriage : till this be
past nothing will be acted. I ame affrayed y<sup>t</sup> betwixt stooles—I
begg of your Lo. to let me hav your counsell and orders heirin
whither his Majestie our maistre hav use for me or not befor I
undertake any thing to chocq our nation or below myself. I rather
renonce all and goe fere abroad.

The Queen hath told publicqly heir to several of the French
grandes y<sup>t</sup> the King hath made me governeur of Dunkerk. I know
not fro whom her Maiestie hath it.

Beggs most humbly pardon for, my Lord,
Your Lo. most humble, most obedient, most
obliged serviteur,
RETORFORT.

---

### LORD RUTHERFORD TO THE EARL OF LAUDERDALE.

MY LORD, [beg. April, 1661.] 23116, f. 5.
Yesterday my man pairted with your Lo: coffres. I wisch they
come to a good port, for this day news cometh y<sup>t</sup> on all hands

robberies are committed be the cavaliers y$^t$ wer disbanded without moneys or recompense, which hath so desesperated them y$^t$ they attacque all they meit with. I hav used all diligence to let your Lo. hav them in tyme as also all necessarie precaution, soe my man is gone w$^t$ them on the chassemaree[a] to Calais. I will not sleip sound till I hear of them frō thence.

I hav given him instructions how to doe at his landing, and a letter to Mr. Burnet at Heth,[b] ane other to Mr. Touris, the searcher at Dover, at the signe of the Prince of Orange, to keip them up and not let them be visited till orders come frō your Lo. as belonging to your Lo. All things are very dear heir be reason of the great number of buyers for the coronation.

My Lord Ormond and others will find theirs very dear passing be the hands of merchands and taylors. I daresay I hav saved something to your Lo.[c] thoe I find all very dear, for I did buy all myself w$^t$ ready money, which hath so incensed the taylors y$^t$ heirafter if your Lo. hav any commissions for me you will be pleased not to astrict me to any in particular, but let me choyse my man.

I send heirin a little memoire of what is in the coffres. I hav not got Mr. Kinloch's compts for the faschion and garniture of your Lo. cloaths, which sall cause the compts be differd at this tyme. Kisses most humbly your Lo. hands, and be your Lo. permission, my Lady Countesss, and my Lady Mary's,

My Lord,

Your Lo. most humble most obedient serviteur,

RETORFORT.

(Enclosed with 23116, f. 5.)

23116, f. 7.     In the coffre for my Lord ane sute w$^t$ black cloak lyned w$^t$ velvet chamared, w$^t$ breeches chamared, garnisched with bleu rubans, and the doublet brocurd dor chamared, lyned with whyt satin.

---

[a] Fishing smack.            [b] Hythe [?].

[c] During the early part of his career Lauderdale was comparatively needy.

A sute of rich oliv-coloured stuff chamared w$^t$ a rich gold dental cartison, the cloak lyned w$^t$ a cloath of gold and silk sutable, the breaches chamared, also garnisched w$^t$ a cherie-colored ruban.

Two pair of gloves of dogg leather deiply parfumed, garnisched according to the sutes, a bever very good and lairge w$^t$ a gold hate band, a boderier of gold and black fond, w$^t$ a sword or couteau of silver guilded sett with turquois, and a base blade, but damasced and musqued.

Their are 4 bands w$^t$ two pair band strings rich, wheirof on is very rich; of the other three your Lo. may choyse and leav the other two for Mr. Mercer. The bands I say will mount to 400$^{li}$, the two best, yea the on cost 285$^{li}$ 10$s$. w$^t$ the handcuffs. This is the dearest merchandise.

### For my Lady Countess.

A black goune of Venetien stuff, w$^t$ two paire of gloves and garnitures conforme, and two musqued eventailes.

### For my Lady Mary.

A goun of coloured brocard, w$^t$ a petticoat of whyt satin faschioned in chamarrure of the new mode, w$^t$ two paire gloves and garniture, and two eventails conforme.

### In a sappin boxe or coffre.

A little boxe with 12 little phiales of Essence of Roses and six of Jessemin. Ane other w$^t$ a silver little box guilded, set w$^t$ turquois (good or bode), full of eau d'ange, and half a douzen bottels of essence of orange; a bigg bottell of water of flower of orange, a bigg boxe of fyne pomode w$^t$ jessemin poudre, a paire of very great tables or trick-track, w$^t$ 4 rame of paper and musqued waxe and black waxe, w$^t$ ane escritoire as was desyred.

For Sir Robert Morray.

A black sute of Venetienne brode plain doubled w$^t$ velvet, garnisched w$^t$ black salined rubans and dogg, musqued gluffs conforme.

Their are a sute of cloaths for Mr. Mercer, w$^t$ sword and belt and feathers and perruque, and garniture conforme, w$^t$ two bands, as your Lo. will leav to him.

---

### LORD RUTHERFORD TO THE EARL OF LAUDERDALE.

23116, f. 74.  MY LORD,

I arryved heir yesternicht and hav schowen my Commission under the Royal Seal, his Maiesties lettre to me, and M. Secretarie Morice's. The Governeur hath delt most civilly with me and is ready to resigne the chairge, only desyrs for his own dischairge y$^t$ as his Maiestie hes been pleased to wryt to me to receav and take the place in my hands, so his Maiestie will be pleased lykwayes to wryt to him y$^t$ he may delyver it to me, and on sayd of this lettre or ordre being for his dischairge he will immediatly after resigne.

Meantyme he is to schow me and giv accompt of all the munition, artillerie, and other materials belonging to the place. I sall begg of your Lo. to sollicit his Maiestie y$^t$ w$^t$ all diligence the ordre may be sent to Sir Edward Harley, for he tells me himself y$^t$ at his pairting fro Court some ten dayes agoe his Maiestie did tell him of my coming, and y$^t$ he sould hav at Dunkerke his Ma. directions for resigning.

Your Lo. will be pleased to remember to send me a cyphre w$^t$ the key.

I ame advysed be Sir Edward to desyre y$^t$ in my Commission (wheiras it is sayd to the Governeur of Dunderk w$^t$ command of all the forces, forts, and strenths their-to belonging) it may be specified of Mardik fort Royal and all others which I begg of your Lo. may be told to the Secretaire Morice to be inserted in my Commission under the Great Seal.

My Lord,

Your Lo. most humble most obedient serviteur,

RETORFORT.

Dunkerke, 30 May, 1661.

LORD RUTHERFORD TO THE EARL OF LAUDERDALE.

MY LORD, 23116, f. 78.

At my arryval heir Sir Edward Harley did send ane express to his Maiestie, and be his means I did wryt to your Lo. He hath gotten a returne frō his Ma$^{tie}$ to surrender me dunkerk, wheirof I ame in possession, but I hav had no news of your Lo.

However, my most noble Lord, I sall begg of your Lo: to be kynd and gratious to this noble cavalier. Sir Edward, of whom I hav receaved great and reall civilities, and who will sympathise w$^t$ your Lo: both in point of policie and religion, for he is a most honest wyse gentleman.

And in case my commission under the great seal of England be not as yet expected suffer me, my Lord, to begg y$^t$ it may hav the same termes and latitude y$^t$ Sir Edward's had, specifying both ports, forts, and strenths, and mardyk and others in particular. If your Lo. secretaire, Mr. James, will be pleased to doe me this grace I hope your Lo. will ordain him to doe it. I expect w$^t$ impatience your Lo. instructions and ordres. Kisses most humbly your Lo. hands.

My Lord,

Your Lo. most humble most obedient serviteur,

RETORFORT.

Dunkerk, 8 Juin, 61.

Dunkerk, 18 7bre, 1661.

23116, f. 128.    I did wryt a long confused piece to my Lord Lauderdaile last
weik amongst others my grievances on was about the sending
over Sir Philip Monkton heir to be controlleur to my preiudice and
affront, if he sculd hav the latitud he pretends.

And becaus I hear now my Lord is indisposed, and $y^r$ for not to
be importuned, and $y^t$ the sayd Sir Philipp is pairted frō this
yesternicht for London not weell satisfyed $w^t$ me, no mor as I ame
with him I must hav recours to you to imploy my Lords credit
and your oun to keip me frō Sir Ph. his bade impressions of me to
my Lord Tresorier Southampton or any els, and $y^r$ for first remitting
you to $y^t$ pairt of my Lord's lettre to instruct you concerning Sir
Phil. and his chairge, I sall next giv you ane accompt of the rest.

Sir Philipp Monkton it seimeth is a favorit of my Lord Treso-
riers hath obtained a patent to be controlleur of the customes heir,
to which I have nothing to gainsay, but be vertew of his patent
pretends to hav a general inspection in all business and to reduce
and bring in the droits of the governour into the King's tresorie,
a thing never practised be any befor in the tyme of any governour,
Spaniard, French, or Inglisch, and since it hath pleased his Maiestie
to giv me a patent not only to inioy what any of my predecessours
had, but what they ought to hav if any thing be omitted, I cannot
without jealousie of ane affront to me or my nation suffer any
novelties come in upon me to crye down my authoritie heir, which
is every day a brauling too the malignant humors of the old ill
principled officers, who as they abhorr as they call it arbitrarie
power, so if they get their will the King sall never be absolut
maistre heir nor will I undertak to command and assure the place
on $y^t$ accompt.

It is trew the King is maistre, and I ame ready when he com-

mands to resigne not only any interest but the chairge of gouverneur yea to expose my lyf for his service, but for others to get patents be surpryse to my preiudice in things wheirof my predecessors hav all bein possessors and never troubled theirin this is of hard digestion. Au pis aller, if my Lord Tresorier will hav all in on the King's accompt, which I ame confident his Maiestie doeth not intend, I can be as answerable my self as any els to giv accompt, and on pain of my body, confiscation of goods, and all els, give full satisfaction and safe the expenses and chairges of a supranumerarie officers.

The particular disput is about a droit heir called the brewers' gulden. Col. Lockart and Sir Rob. Harley have inioyed it, and yet I must be questioned. It is enouch I ame a Scot, yea thoe I never received a pennie of the sayd droit and yt I ame not so avaritious to prey having few or non successors to my tresors.

If you can doe any thing heirin during my Lord's indisposition, act as you think fitt.

The King promised me at pairting y^t no commission nor patent sould be given in dunkerk w^tout my advyse or advertisment. Heir is a new creation be surpryse, all others Governours inioyed what they incroach upon in my tyme. I ame as ready as willing and w^tout vanitie able to rendre compt as any of them my predecessours. Why treat me thus I hav done.

Your own man.

---

LORD RUTHERFORD TO THE EARL OF LAUDERDALE.

MY LORD,                    Dunkerk, 23 7^{ber}, 1661.    23116, f. 130.

I was overioyed at the recept of your Lo. the other day. Your Lo. sall not want a sogers prayers for your health becaus I ame so much interessed therein.

Your coach will be ready next moneth.    Let me know if I sall cause put on your armes or if your Lo. will not hav her, for I will make use myself als, and y^r for let me ones mor hav your Lo. armes with the colours for I hav lost the former.

I must recommend the bearer heirof to your Lo. Lieut. Col. Knichtly; he is a very prettie gallant gentleman, most necessare for this Garnison, he is casseird be a Court Martial heir.   Thoe be vertew of my authoritie I could remitt him, yet I rather hav it from his Maiestie, be an lettre and ordre to me to receav and rehabilitat him again his Maiestie having pardoned him he will giv your Lo. an accompt of alle, and truely he is not so criminel as they make him; had he don it in France he had never bein called to a Court Martial, but bein reconciled without much pain. Ones mor I recommend him to your Lo. to sollicite for him with his R. H. to whom I hav made my supplications too in his behalf.

Since your Lo. commands me to tell you what was layed out for your Lo. in france I sall say freely I have not tyme to cast upp the compts exactly, but I conceav it will amount to two hundred and betwixt twentie fyv and threetie punds sterling.

I begg y^t your Lo mak no hast, but when your Lo. is resolved to giv it to Mr. Willschaw Scots, Merchands.

My Lord,
Your Lo. most humble most obedient serviteur,
RUTHERFURD.

---

## LORD RUTHERFORD TO THE EARL OF LAUDERDALE.

23116, f. 148. MY LORD,                    Dunkerk, 6 9^br, 1661.
                                                        27 8:

At the very houre I receaved your Lo. with your Lo. seal of armes and colours, your coach arryved heir, for I had sent ane Cap^tn to Bruxelles, who brocht it be land be four horses from thence;

it would hav bein spoyled be water as they informed me, and would hav coast as much be reason of frequent changing of boats they say the coach is cheap but I find it dear. All the nails of harnois and coach are double guilded, their are six harnois w$^t$ the postillons sadles. If it doe not fit your Lo. I sall take it back again for it will cost nothing the transportation having sent this hoys express. It comes to 1700$^{ll}$ permission silver, and twentie four crounes for the bringing, with 8 crounes for other little compts, making in all (as they compt to me) ane hundred seventie on pund, fyf schilens ster. nay if it pleas not your Lo. and y$^t$ any other will hav it, I hav set the pryce for y$^t$ end, for els I sould not compt so exactly with your Lo.

I sall hav the honor to wryt to your Lo. be the next ordinare and giv ane accompt of all things heir. I have constantly 700 men at work yet advanceth but slowly. Rome was not built in on day.

My Lord,
Your Lo. most humble most obedient servant,
RUTHERFURD.

I send your Lo. a piece of new wyn of daye, [?] it is entiere rare heir, and nou cometh this way; when I find any good your Lo. sall hav pairt.

---

MY LORD, Dunkerk, 13 9$^{bre}$, 1661. 23116, f. 150.

I ame advertised by his grace my Lord of Albemarle y$^t$ Sir Rob. Harley's regiment is destined for Tangiers and sould pairt from hence schortly; if they get not their decompts and arriers they will make a hurlie burlie, or a richt doun mutinie, and the poor scot may suffer.

If England wer farther frō us heir I would be mor a tease and securitie. Never officers loved their countrey so weill as ours heir doeth, for I beleiv giv them their pay and let them stay in England they would hardly weary many of them, yea our very ingenier thoo a Dutch mate hath left me in the heat of our business, but I forgiv him. Many of our officers are sick heir and mor as the tienth of our sogers payeth tribut with sickness. I dare not tell how I am keipt in hot water heir, only beleiv me my good Lord je ne suis pas icy pour casser des noix. Pray God make me and continue me a loyal fidel subiect and creature to his Majestie.

I intend to sell my coach mears and three Spanish horse I hav heir, on my word of honor botht with the French kings moneys, of whom since my pairting I hav gotten 10,000<sup>lb</sup> currant. If your Lo. hav a mynd for the 7 coach gray dapled mears, I sall send them over; if not and y<sup>t</sup> any of your court hav a mynd for them and my horses I sall send them on your Lo: advertisement, it is too much macquinioned [?] begs most humbly pardon for

My Lord,

Your Lo. most humble most obedient servant,

RUTHERFURD.

---

LORD RUTHERFORD TO THE EARL OF LAUDERDALE.

23116, f. 155.  MY LORD,                        Dunkerk, ₁⁵⁄₂₅ 9<sup>bre</sup>, 1661.

The Doctor General of this garnison is dead, thoe I hav the power to place ane other, yet because Doctor Burnet (on whom I hav cast my eyes for his abilities rather as his relations to me) being a Scot, and fearing to giv ether subject or appearence of jealousie to the garnison y<sup>t</sup> two Bretheren Burnets, both Scots and of my relations, sould have chairge and direction of soul and bodie over the Inglisch heir.   Theirfor doe I supplicat your Lo. that his Ma^tie may be intressed in it, that the commission for the sayd chairge may come frō the secretaire his Majestie, and your Lo. hav the thanks and acknowledgement only my consent attached becaus this was the treatie betwixt Sir Edward Nicolas and me about the creation of any officer.   This is the humble requeist of,

My Lord,

Your Lo. most humble most obedient servant,

RUTHERFURD.

---

### LORD RUTHERFORD TO THE EARL OF LAUDERDALE.

MY LORD,                            Dunkerk, ⅟⅟ 9^bre, 1661.    23116, f. 165.

Not having receaved any ordres of your Lo. of a long time, I hoped my man sould bring me some whose arryval without a lettre frō your Lo. did a little trouble me, supposing it was be his cairlesness.

I intended to hav sent in a little paper to your Lo. a memoire of some things to be presented to his Ma. but being certainly informed be M. de Puij, the Duk's valet de chambre, y^t his H. R. will be heir this nicht, I will not trouble your Lo. he being on the place to take connoisance.   I have written a letter to Sir Will. Waller in his son's behalf.   I sall plainly tell your Lo. he is not fitt for this service or trade, he may prove other.   It is not but he is very honest, dcutifull, and willing, but their is something wanting.   I hav written so categorically to his father y^t whatever he desyrs sould be done I sall obey, thoe to my preiudice and others.   I sall desyre your Lo. with all secrecie to let me know if the cloaths y^t cometh over heir to the King's regt. be payed be his Maiestie, or if the regt. must pay for them.

Becaus my L. Wentworth sends me ordres or word to send him over the moneys y$^t$ is due in arrieres to that reg$^t$ be reason of the payement must be made for them cloaths at London. This is most iust in y$^t$ case, and if the King pay for them I think as iust he may dispose of those moneys, for he is not rich enouch to giv in all and all, and to hav so many Iron in the fyre to me it is all on, for I have the moneys. It would help heir the fortifications when moneys lacketh. I begg your Lo. service, kisses most humbly your Lo. hands.

My Lord,<br>Your Lo. most humble most obedient servant,<br>RUTHERFURD.

---

LORD RUTHERFORD TO THE EARL OF LAUDERDALE.

23116, f. 168.  MY LORD,

I receaved two of your Lo. at ones, next day after his H. Royal was pairted frō hence, whose arryval as it did surpryse us no less did his sudden depairture deiect us. He was pleased to leave ordres for the modelling and ranking the companies of those regts. destined for Tangiers. Our Scots regt. of Neubruch is reduced to two companies, and they cast in to ane Irisch reg. Sir James Hamilton's sonn commandeth on of the companies. It is not my pairt (because too much interessed) to say y$^t$ his Maiestie having so many Englisch reg. on foot, and four Irisch regts. with his H. R. micht have on poor Scots regt. I ame sorry his Maiestie sould hav promised anything to Doctor Burnet, but it floweth frō his unparalelld bountie to accord to all what men desyr. This is a little ruffle to me so much the more sensible, becaus my own lieut.-col. without my knowledge did wryt over to M. Halsey, cupbearer, to sollicit

the chairge of Doctor for y<sup>t</sup> man Vial, as also heir at Dunkerk
w<sup>t</sup>out my knowledge did sollicit his H. R. I will not say it is
ingratitude in him, but Dieu m'en garde des ces gens cij peice and
piece they will wear me out of all authoritie. Pardon, my Lord,
this digression.

Never any sets forward this way but it is to put me out of Dunkerk. Sir Will. Compton was the man in his tyme, and now my
Lord Gerald, who sould have comed with the Duke, my Lord
Tresorer, and Lord Roberts will hav me out. What a poxe w<sup>t</sup> permission aileth the world to persecut so a poor Scots body. God
save the King, and make me a constant loyal subiect, even to spend
my heart blood for him, thoe he sould chass me away.

My Lord,
Your Lo. most humble, most reall, and obedient servant,
RUTHERFORD.

Dunkerk, 6 X<sup>bre</sup>, 1661.

---

### LORD RUTHERFORD TO THE EARL OF LAUDERDALE.

MY LORD,                                                    23116, f. 173.

I receaved your Lo. of the 10<sup>th</sup> instant, which sould make me
proud be the relating of his Maiesties most kynd and charitable
expressions towards me. I pray God keip me allwayes constant
and loyal. I will bragg no mor. I hav merited least of any of his
subiects and creatures. On thing I must communicat to your Lo.
y<sup>t</sup> wer it not his Ma. service in a most particular way to be heir in
conscience and point of honour, I sould be presently wearied of the
imploy. I hav 4000 spyes about me, and nou I dare impart myself
too, since he that was confident hath acted against me and the
principles of freindschipp. I must confess that I make profit of this

strait, it makes me mor circumspect and goe the cheirfuller for the King's service, teste elevee malgre l'envie.

Because this year is at ane end, and I have many compts of the garnison on my hands to dischairge myself, and let my Lord Tresorer and others see y$^t$ sogers may be frugal, honest, and able to menage. I sall beg of your Lo. that his Ma$^{tie}$ will permitt me to come over for 8 dayes only to rendre compt to his Ma. or my Lord Tresorer (but be his Ma. special ordre alenerly*), of my recepts and despenses heir for this garnison. If it be graunted it must be speidily, for we must beginn to hasten our new works with the new year. I expect with impatience the honor of your Lo. return to this prayer.

My Lord,
Your Lo. most humble most obedient servant,
RUTHERFURD.

Dunkerk, ⁺⁺ X$^{bre}$ [1661].

---

## LORD RUTHERFORD TO THE EARL OF LAUDERDALE.

23117, f. 59. MY LORD,            Dunkerk, 26 Jun. 1662.

I hav vowed (beggerly to) to importun your Lo. till I get my ansuer. The subiect theirof be your Lo. weilfaire in body, Court, and State, and my being in your Lo. good graces I told be my precedent in a prophetique humor y$^t$ a body of our own C.$^b$ men would prov usefull heir and not chairgeable.

I had ane lettre of his Grace of Albemarle last day with ane inclosed petition which had bein presented to the Counsell, signed be several officers reduced of Dunkerk. I know not how you relisch those petitions signed in England be so many sogers hands, having

* Only            $^b$ Country.

bein all at their several homes and theirfor behoved to hav a rendevous to doe it, but wheir I hav bein bred it would hav passed for richt down mutinie.  God giv us all as much of honestie and loyaltie as I see we hav of interest.  Then sall his Ma^{tie} be happie in his subiects.

My Lord,

Your Lo. most humble most obedient servant,

RUTHERFURD.

----

LORD RUTHERFORD TO THE EARL OF LAUDERDALE.

MY LORD,                                    [No date.]    23117, f. 76.
   I hav reason to suspect your Lo. silence, the rather that I ame informed some good godly soules had dreamd and vented in Ingland or your Court that this place was to be betrayed to the frenches be my muschipe, yea some of our oun countrey peers contributed with their good opinions to the same.  God rewaird them all.  I sall not be obliged to burne Dianar's temples.  They will save me those paines.  Our trouppes for Tangers are embarqued, all well satisfyed with me and I most satisfyed with them.
   I hav advertised his Maiestie be Secretarie Nicolas that the report is heir that M. de Caracene* is in arrest be M. de Marsine.  May be yow know mor and sooner as I doe heirof.  My Lord, thoe your Lo. doe not honour me with your commands, be not affrayed of me, I beseich your Lo.  In good earnest I hope to proof steal to the back.  God make every subiect alyk.

My Lord,

Your Lo. most humble most obedient servant,

RUTHERFURD.

----

* Spanish ambassador at the Hague.

## LORD RUTHERFORD TO THE EARL OF LAUDERDALE.

23117, f. 84.      MY LORD,                          Dunkerk, 21 7ᵇʳᵉ, s. v. 1662.

I receaved your Lo. of the 18th with the inclosed, to both which I returne ane succinct ansuer, being surprysed and galled at the contents theirof.[a]  I hav ever professed to be your Lo. most in all obliged servant, and now if I wer not touched with your concerns, and hazard all that is dear to me for them, I sould prov but a scholem[b] and a farfarr.  I signify but little in this world, but what I ame good for I begg your Lo. will make use of, for still I say I ame most perfectly,

My Lord,
Your Lo.
A vendre et dependre.

I ame affrayed that my designe on teviotdaill will prov ridiculous. God keip me from it if you continue so at home—I mean Scotland. It will be better to supp a french potage neir orleans.

---

## LORD RUTHERFORD TO THE EARL OF LAUDERDALE.

23117, f. 88.      MY LORD,                          Dunkerk, 3 8ᵇʳᵉ, 1662.

I receaved your Lo. of the 27 7ᵇʳᵉ, as I hav receaved the lettres wheirof your Lo. wryts, so hav I returned ane ansuer to that freind with ane other inclosed which I hope are safely comed to hands.

For my proiect in Teviotdaill I sall not be very instant in the sollicitations till it be fairer weather.

[a] Probably Lauderdale had written to him regarding the Billeting Conspiracy.
[b] Schelm.

But for my pass to France I hav got it at such a tyme that I ame quyt disoriented and to giv your Lo. accompt yrof I sall begg your Lo. patience and attention for a little. Their hath runn a bruit heir neir this moneth of the reddition or exchange of Dunkerk, every day confirmed frō all places (safe Whythall) with all imaginable appearences of truth. I did wryt to Sir Edward Nicolas theirupon to know his Ma. will and pleasure, answered it was yᵗ their was no such matter.* Yet last day I see a lettre frō the Maior of Graveline, saying in positiv terms yᵗ Mr. d'Estraches was Governeur of Dunkerk and M. de Belfont in his place of Graveline. This I confess alarmed me, wheirupon I did wryt to Sir Edward again and inclosed ane narrativ of all business heir to be schouen to his Ma. containing the inconvenients may arryes be concealing it frō me (en tel cas). I expect every moment news theirof.

Last nicht the same reconfirmed be a letter frō Count de Charrois in doun richt terms, yea Batillier the sec. il embassade, passing last day at Calais frō Paris, told he had the contract signed be his Ma. of France. This is knowen to all the officers and sogers, who are in a most deip consternation. This begets a contempt of me in all their spirits, either yᵗ I conceal the veritie, or yᵗ I ame not worthie it sould be communicated; whatever be the matter, provyded it be for his Ma. weil, I ame aboundantly satisfyed. It wer too tedious to tell your Lo. the number of inconvenients following thir news, but in particular all my measurs are broken for the next year's proiect, and had I knowen only 20 dayes agoe (if it be trew) I had saved his Maiestie neir 2500ˡⁱ ster.

Now, my dear Lord, most pressingly I supplicat your Lo. with all hast let me to know in particular of his Ma. if it be so or not, and how I sall behav myself, for at present I signifye little heir in the opinion of all. Most cheirfully sall I retyre, and wheirever his

* The first mention in Pepys of this transaction is Oct. 19, 1662. The charge for maintaining this garrison had greatly increased under Rutherford's management, amounting to 120,000ℓ. a-year.

Ma. service call me, runn and hazard for it the best of my blood till their be no mor. God bless his Ma. with all felicities, and in particular with wyse and fidel counsellors.

>Pardon, my Lord,
>>Your Lo. most humble, most obedient servant,
>>>RUTHERFURD.

---

## LORD RUTHERFORD TO THE EARL OF LAUDERDALE.

MY LORD,                                            Doil, 27 April, 1663.

This nicht we schipp all in with a resolution to pairt to-morrow. I hav the reserv his Ma^{ties} schipp w^t me and three other loadned w^t sogers and munition. Their are tuo behind in the river, and so ame forced to leav them with 100 sogers to wait on Sir Jhon Lauson or ane other convoye. I hav nether my commis nor instructions nor the Establischment, nor my old compts of Dunkerk closed with a quietus est, yet to serv his Ma^{tie} I goe most willingly. I wisch we could flye, he is so good a maistre their is pleasur to serv him weill. God giv me the grace and force to doe it till my last breath.

[Torn away.]

to be recommended to the Embassadeur particularly.

Next to advertise his Ma^{tie} y^t I may hav a secret ordre for keiping up a Scots companie and cap. in Col. Geraldin's reg^t, becaus befor ever his own reg^t was in the King's service my Lord Neuburg's was, and it is iust, if not the reg^t at least on companie be keipt up. I hav done. God preserv yow long, y^t I may hav the confort of your freindschipp. I sall provyd your Lo: w^t a M[?] for Mr. Jean and a Lyon for Prince Rupert. To your Lo. and all those y^t honor yow. I ame most really,

>>My Lord.

[Torn away.]

## LORD TEVIOT TO THE EARL OF LAUDERDALE.

MY BEST OF LORDS,                                       23120, f. 42.

Since my pairting frō England the 28 Apryl we hav seen the
ennemy tuo tymes in great bodyes and w$^t$ him spoke. We built
fyv redouts of stone and lyme, whither he would or not, and afterwards made peace, concluding it on the head of his armie, he and
I sitting in two chaires. It is only for six moneths and to cur
King's pleasure herein w$^t$ intention to giv him accompt of all. I
pairted frō Tanger the 27 Agust, leaving it in good ordre w$^t$ 9
moneths provisions, abondance of merchandise. I passed throw the
kingdome of Algarves, kissed the King of Portugal's hands at
Lisbone, arryved at Portsmouth the 16 7$^{bre}$, wheir I had the honor
to kiss the Duk and Dutchess hands, frō thence came to the Baith,
kissed their Ma$^{ties}$ hands and Sir R. Morray and passed be Chichester,
wheir was the Earle of Middleton$^a$ and Neubourg,$^b$ kissed the Chan-
cellour's hands at Corneberry, and now iust now arryv at London.

Now since your Lo. hath given me the libertie to be saucie and
too familiar, I sall make a humble petition to your Lo. y$^t$ yow will
favorise me in the purchase of Rutherfurd, be persuading the owner
to pairt w$^t$ it in just and reasonable termes. I will take no advan-
tage on him, but submitt myself to tuo freinds whatever they judge
the valeur of a land without ane house, holding ward not seigneur
of the church, according to its rents I ame content to pay. I hav
written to my Lords Bellenden and Whytkirk to make their
addresses to your Lo. about this subject. I intend to pairt w'in a
moneth at fardest to come kiss your Lo. hands in Scotland. The

---

$^a$ Royal Commissioner for Scotland from 1660 to the summer of 1663, when the
rivalry between him and Lauderdale ended in the victory of the latter. He succeeded
Lord Teviot at Tangiers.

$^b$ Lauderdale's competitor for the Scotch secretaryship: appointed captain of the
King's Guards. He was in strict alliance with Middleton, and came with him to
Court after the failure of the Billeting Conspiracy.

King pairted yesterday frō Baiths. Dynes on Wednesday at Corneberry, wheir the Duk meits him and cometh y^t nicht to Oxford,
wheir he is to stay 7 dayes.

My best Lord,

Your Lo. petit valet,

TEVIOT.

London, 22 7^bre, 1663.

———————

LORD TEVIOT TO THE EARL OF LAUDERDALE.

23120, f. 57.   MY BEST OF LORDS,

I waited at York on his Grace and your Lo. coming, but when I
learned that yow pairted frō Newcastel yesterday I came this lenth
thinking to find your Lo. heir or at Alerton, but Mr. Mackie [a]
incertain what way yow are to come and affrayed to miss I giv
your Lo. thè trouble of this, begging most humbly pardon if I
wait no longer on his G. or your Lo. My tyme prescryved for
my returne is so schort y^t I will hardly adiust my business w^t it.
Your Lo. hath many ennemys, at least envyers at Court, and I lyk
you all the better for it. God's blessing on yow. I leav yow to
Sir Rob. for those things.

The Duke of Buckinghame professeth much freindschip to yow
and told me the same y^t yow had illwischers. I hope you will
thryv the better. I kissed the King's hands on Thursday at 11 of
the clock coming out frō the Queen's bed chamber. Very sade
Her Ma^tie abandoned be all and speechles; when I pairted schee was
not dead but without miracle depairted y^t nicht or next morning.

If his G. or your Lo. hav forgot anything in Scotland or on the
waye let me have your ordres. Thoe I did kiss my Lady Countesses
hands at Highgate and got regales w^t Sir Ro: yet hearing your

———

[a] A confidential servant of Lauderdale, often employed in carrying despatches to
and from Scotland.

Lo. to be on the way hither I did not receav her commands at pairting.

My best of Lords,

Your Lo. petit valet,

TEVIOT.

Borrowbridge, 27 8^bre, 1663.

---

LORD TEVIOT TO THE EARL OF LAUDERDALE.

MY BEST OF LORDS,        Tanger, 24 Jan. 166⅜.    23121, f. 33.

We arryved safe at this place the 14th instant with the loss of 9 horses. I hav payed for them all but ame not sure as yet how to be reimbursed. Our deputie governour fearing my stay in England had continued the peace for two moneths, but becaus I intend to make our new fortifications which is contraire to our peace already made, I ame of opinion we sall break, for work I must and hav advertised Guyland. The Kent fregat, Cap. Teileman, will bring your Lo. a pype of Cery wyn and some orange waters,

My best of Lords,

Your Lo. most humble and most obedient valet,

TEVIOT.[*]

Our deputie Governeur hath acted with great prudence in my absence, we are most entyre, and I begg your Lo. will be kynd to his at his arryval.

Earle Lauderdaill.

---

EARL OF ROTHES TO THE EARL OF LAUDERDALE.

MY DEAR LORD,        Julay the 6 [1665.]    23123, f. 120.

I am much trublid that by the courts remuffal it uill be impossibell for you to leat me hear so oftin ffrom, bot I most intreat ffor it als oftin as posiblie you can. The taym ffor the conuensioun dus nou

[*] He remained in charge of Tangiers until his death in a skirmish with the Moors, 1665.

draue nier, and I shall by the nixt post or tuo giff you acaunt of
uhat I shall in all humilatie expeckt ffrom his Majestie as letiers or
instruxions in relasion to the conuensione. You may remember a
great uhayl ago his Majestie did in a prayffit letier ureatun by your
Lo. comand me to retard the leues of the ffranshe ofisiers undier my
Lord jorge duglies, of thos thrie hunder men uhich hie brought
a uarant ffor. I uas tu long of geating the comand ffor me to meack
a stop bot that it uold have esalie bin perseued, and tho I haue
indeuoried it to put all the stop I could prayfitlie yit I ffaynd thay
uill be in redines aganst the tuintiethe of this munthe, ffor thay ar
uerie dilieant ouer the kingdum, and the ships uill be hear presislie
aganst that day sent by the ffrenshe king ffor transporting of them,
so that I most expeck a positiff comand uhat I shall du, ffor iff a
stop be put to them it uill in my opinion be luckt upon as a breathe
and the considerasion of that meacks me not enou uhat to du, bot
iff ther be not a spidie breath layck to be I shuld thinck so small a
number of men is not much uirthe of being notified, bot leat me
haue an ansuier to this als sun as you can, and so ffor this post adeaie
my dear Lard,

[ROTHES.]

---

LORD GEORGE DOUGLAS TO THE EARL OF LAUDERDALE.

23124, f. 11.     Since that our kings ambassadeur hes takin his leuve of this court,
and that it is thothit that ther shall be wars betuixt his Majesté and
the king of France,[a] I wold intrait thet faveur of your Lo. as to
assour his Majesté of my most faithfull loyalnesse and all the
regiments that I dow command, as also that I might know what is
his Majestes will that I should dow, for altho as your Lo. dis know
that I have nothing in my ouin contray and no other livlyhod but

* In 1666 France was in alliance with Holland.

be my regiment hier, yet whatever commands his Majesté will honnor me and my regiment with shall be most punctuall and faithually obyed ; as your Lo. hes alweis doun me the honneur as to be my frind I hop you will continued now and lat me know what is the kings intention we should dow. I should wish that your Lo. wold lat me hier from you as soun as possibl can, for I belive I may may be commanded to go towards jttallie or cattalloing. I begge your Lo. will excusse me for this fridom I tak as to give you this trouble, since I am most really,

My Lord,

Your Lo. most humbl and obedient servint,

DOUGLAS.

Paris, 9 Janvir, 1666[6⅚].

---

LORD HOLLES (English Ambassador at Paris) TO THE EARL OF LAUDERDALE.

MY LORD,       Paris, ¹⅟₄ February [16]6⅚.    23124, f. 69.

This is but to acknowledge the receite of your Lo$^{ps}$ letter and to present you with my most humble service, for my Lord Douglas doth himself give your Lo$^p$ an account of the little which wee both of us yet know will be done in his busines as to the transporting of his regiment, of which some difficulty as yet seemes to be made here ; by the next post more may be knowen, of which he or I or both will give your Lo$^p$ an account. In the meane time lett me begg the continuance of your Lo$^{ps}$ favor to esteeme me as I really am,

My Lord,

Your Lo$^{ps}$ most humble servant,

HOLLES.

THIERRY CHARPENTIER (Secretary to Marquis of Louvois) TO
LORD GEORGE DOUGLAS.

23124, f. 70.    MONSIEUR,        A St. Germain en laye, le 2 Mars, 1666.

J'ay pris les ordres de monseigneur le Marquis de Louvois sur ce
qui vous regarde. Votre regiment doibt estre assemblé a St.
Quentin et estre embarqué a St. Vallery. Je travailleray des demain
a ce qui est a faire pour faire rendre toutes vos comp[agnie]s a St.
Quentin, mais vous scavez, Monsieur, qu'elles ne peuvent partir des
quartiers ou elles sont qu'elles n'yayent esté remplacées. Ainsy je
ne croy pas qu'elles puissent estre avant trois sepmaines icy? toutes
ensemble. Je ne perdray aucun moment de temps a ce que je doibt
faire en cette occasion. Et je cheriray toujours beaucoup celles qui
me donneront moyen de vous tesmoingner combien je suis,
Monsieur,
Votre tres humble serviteur,
CHARPENTIER.

---

LORD GEORGE DOUGLAS TO EARL OF LAUDERDALE.

23124, f. 72.    MY LORD,        Paris, 3 Marche, 1666.

According as I did wryt to your Lo. by my last, the King of
France has given me my pass conforme to our capitulation, and as
your Lo. will si by the enclosed which I have just now recevid
from Monsieur de Louvois, his secretaire, we ar to be embarqued
at St. Vallery, so your Lo. most be plaissed to send the passes for
the wessells that will transporte us from thence. I cannot spessefie
the number so your Lo. most procure passes for such wessells as

shall serve for the transpotation of the regiment. By my last I dissaired your Lo. to let me know in what place the king dissaired we should land at ; now that yow dow know the place that we ar to be imbarqued at your Lo. will be plaised to lat me know his Majesties plaiser in it, which shall be punctually observid, wind and wather serving. St. Quentin, which is the place of our randevous, is six days' march from St. Wallery, and it will be thri weiks before we can be ther, so it will be the last of this month before we can be imbarqued. My Lord Holles dis pairt from this, he dis tell me with in ten or tualve days; so, my Lord, what letters yow dow send to me efter his pairting, addresse them under a cover, A Monsieur, Monsieur Richard, maistre de la poste d'Anglettere. I am with respect, my Lord,

Your Lo. most humbl and obedient servint,

DOUGLAS.

---

LORD GEORGE DOUGLAS TO THE EARL OF LAUDERDALE.

MY LORD,                 Paris, 6 March, 1666.    23124, f. 78.

Sinc my last to your Lo. things ar changed, for now the King of France dis trait us in the most crouel way that ever was, for he hes told me that he has no mony to pay us what is ouing us, and that we shall have our rout according as I did wryt to you by my last, and ships at St. Wallery, but no mony to pay us what is ouing us, that we might pay our debts in the places we ar in, nor to carry us to the seaside. He dis this thinking to make our sojers stay behind and distroy the regiment. I hop this shall not have the effect they belive, for I am assowred non of our sojers will stay, and they should beg ther bred thorow the contray. I beliv ther was never such a crouel and barborus action doun efter so many years services, spending our bleuds and fortuns in his service, to be nessesitate to beg hom, and perhaps putt in prison for my debts, and refuss the payment of our arriers as also my pension. I believe such a traittement as this will be a warning to all my contremen or any of our kings subject. I have sothit my pass presently with our rout that we may go to the sea sid the best way we can, and ships for our transportation according to ther last promis which the secretaire of state said I should have, but that before I but to give him the pasports for the saif retourne of the ships, so my Lord I pray you to lat me have them by the first post, as at so to lat me know what I should dow in this. I refer other particullaires to my Lord Holles letters to your Lo. and my Lord Arlington, only I intrait a spidy and diligent ansur, for befor I can recev it I will presse them, so that I hop to gaitt all my ordres and pass from them, and will pairt immediatly upon any account out of this most ungraitfull countray, wher thy begin to louk now opon me in a most strange way. So expecting with impatiance to hier from your Lo. and to be in Ingland, I dow remaine,

My Lord,

Your Lo. most humbl and obedient servint,

Douglas.

---

LORD GEORGE DOUGLAS TO THE EARL OF LAUDERDALE.

23124, f. 87.  MY LORD,                        Paris, 10 Marche, 1666.

Yesterday I did disaire of the King of France that since he was not plaissed to pay us what he was ouing us, that he would be plaissed to give me immediatly my congé and routté and ordres for my transportation according to his promis to me. He told me, Je vous ay deja ditte que je suis court d'argent pour le present, mais je donné ordre a Monsieur de Louvois de vous donner tous vos

ordres nessesaires, et vous depecher ; and he did immediatly call for
Monsieur de Louvois and commanded him to dispache me, who
told me he should dow it with all diligence, and for that effect the
ordres dis pairt to morrow to . . . . . thri companies marche
that is towards Lorraine. He told me also that we should have
estapes upon our routte, which is so much flech, bred, and drink
for every sojer, and to the officirs a proportion, and that we should
find our shipes redy at St. Wallery for to cairy us over, and as for
our tow months pay which was ouing us and my pension, that the
king wold pay us when he had mony if I would live an officire
behind, so that I had no raison to complaine of the King, and that
he did kip our capitullation to us. The raison why thy dow not
pay us our arriers was that thy thothit that that wold brek the regiment and oblige the officirs to stay, of the which thy ar extraimly
desseved, for we shall cairy over seven hundrid as good sojers as is
in the world ; this is now ther last dessein how thy will traitte us,
which your Lo. may belive for certine, as all so that we shall be
imbarqued against the first of Appryll. Now that I have had my
congé of the King of France I will not si him no mor till I be redy
to pairt for to tak my liv of him. I dow expect with impatiance the
passports for the wessels, for the secretaire told me that befor I went
from court I but to delivre them to him. I told him that it was
litle honnor for the King of France for to reffuse to pay us our
arriers and si us put in prison, or at list striped naked for our debts
in our quarters. His ansur was that the King had a dow[a] with
his monyes, for to riche[b] out shipes to fight against us. I shall
not faill to advertis your Lo. when we marche from St. Quentin,
our lieu d'assamblé, and at our arrivall at St. Wallery, and I hop
your Lo. will pardon me for the trouble I give you by my letters,
and that I am,

My Lord,
Your Lo. most humbl and obedient servint,
DOUGLAS.

LORD GEORGE DOUGLAS TO THE EARL OF LAUDERDALE.

23124, f. 94. MY LORD,                           Paris, ce 13 Mars, 1666.

Immediatly after the wryting of my last the secretaire of state send for me and told me that the King had maid une efort, and had borrowed moneys for to pay us, and that we shall be payed to the day of our embarquement, and at the King's retourne from the reveu at Compienne, wher he is gon this day and will be againe this day agithit [eight] days I should have my orders, so this will retarde us aight or ten days longer nor I expected, but my Lord I shall mak all the heast that can be, and I hop to cairy over a good regiment and at leist seven hundred men, for ther was never men so overjoied and willing as all the officirs and sojers ar.  I asked the secretaire if the king wold not pay me my pensions he was owing me; he told me that he had no ordres from the King to dow it, for it was a particullaire bissinis that regardit myself, and that for the capitullation the king wold kip it, and bad me spik to the king; what he will dow I know not, but I am affrayed of the warsit.  I dow expect with impatience for thos pasports for the wessills as also to know in what place I should land at.  I pray yow my Lo. to lat me know if your Lo. will command me anything hier for your service, for now we have the foire de St. Germaine hier, and I can be abl to cairy over things with me conveniently.  I shall wish to God I may be abl to testifie how much I am your Lo. servint, and sensibl of thos obligations I have to your Lo. and in particullaire in this last, which shall be the greatest passion of him that is with respect,

My Lord,
Your Lo. most humble and most obedient servint,
DOUGLAS.

## LORD GEORGE DOUGLAS TO THE EARL OF LAUDERDALE.

MY LORD,                                    Paris, 24 March, 1666.      23124, f. 105.

At the retourne of the court to St. Germains, I went ther, so yesterday the secretaire of stat told me that he should send presently the ordres for to casse the regiment assembl at St. Quenten, and that he had ordres from the king to command me to rettire me self immediately to my regiment, that the king was not satisfied with me, and that for my pensions the king wold not pay me. I told him that I was ouing a great daill of debt hier and I had not a farding mony; he told me the king wold pay the regiment but as for me not, and that I must be going presently, so my Lord you may juge in what a sad condition I am in. My Lord Ambassadeur hes bein plaised to casse lenne me opon his credit thri hundrid pounds sterling for to pay my debts and to retir myself, so I will pairt within thri or four days for St. Quentin, wher I wold stay till my regiment be assembled. The secretaire of stat told me he should send me what ordres should be nessesaire to me you may jug my Lord how things stand with me hier by this hard usag I recev. I know not if I dar trusit ther promis in what they say they will dow concerning the regiment; therfor my Lord if they should put me aff with delays (as I dow not think thy will) lat me know what I shall dow. I have recevid yesterday the passes for the waissels, but no ordre for my landing nor wher I should dow it. My Lord Ambassadeur does wryt by this post to my Lord Arlington of it, as also to addresse his letteres and ordres for me in our queen mothers pakit, for his Lo. does pairt within tow or thri days, if thy should braik ther words to me hier concerning my regiment. I have told Collonel Gerardin what may be douin in that conjunctur, who will acquaint your Lo. with it. I am,

My Lord,

Your Lo. most humble servint,

DOUGLAS.

LORD GEORGE DOUGLAS TO THE EARL OF LAUDERDALE.

23123, £ 140.  MY LORD,                              Diepe, the 16 Octobre, 1667.

I dow send over this officire for to intraite your Lo. to spik to the King, that his Majestie will be plaised according to his word to me (upon the which I payed my regiment four days pay of my ouin mony) to order me the payment of it, which was four days I stayed longer nor I receved pay for, and his Majestie did assour me I should be payed for it befor the Duke of York, and my Lord Generall told me so to. I dow assour your Lo. that insted of gaining upon this bissinis I will be a grait lousser, for ther was sum personnes that was plaised to mak a reporte go amongst my regiment that I was going for Tangere, so that ther runeaway almost thrie hundred men the day befor I shiped, so that with thos and the sik men I was forced to live be hinde; all that I have broght over is seven hundred and six men in sted of twelve, so that I most repay the superplus, which really my Lord will putt me extraimly to it, what with the weknisse of my regiment, so my Lord I will have nide of the continuatione of your Lo. faveur to spik to the King for me, and if his Majestie wold be plaised to confer that honor upon me that I dissaired your Lo. to spik alredy to his Majesty of, it wold be extraimly for the advanement of my fortune, so if your Lo. thinks fitt to spik againe to the king of it, you will oblige me extraimly in it, and to assure his Majesty that whatever service he hes a dow with me or my regiment I shall obey his commands most faithfully and punctually. I hop your Lo. will pardon me for this trouble I give you, and belive I am,

My Lord,

Your most humbl and obedient servant,

DOUGLAS.

### LORD GEORGE DOUGLAS TO THE EARL OF LAUDERDALE.

MY LORD,                                 Paris, 9 May, 1668.    23129, f. 100.

Now that the peace is maid hier thy ar going a mak a wery great
reforme a mongst the troups, and I am affrayed that it faill havily
upon my regiment, ther for I wold intraitte your Lo. that you wold
be plaised to spik to the King that he wold be plaised to wryt a
latter hier in my faveurs, and also to Sir Jhon Trever to spik to the
King of France and Monsieur de Louvois. If your Lo. will be
plaised to dow me this faveur it must be doun by the first post; for
the reforme of troups ar to be presently doun, so ther is no tyme to
be lost. I shall begg the honnor of your ansur, and to belive I am,

My Lord,
Your Lo. most humbl and most obedient servant,
DOUGLAS.

---

### LORD GEORGE DOUGLAS TO THE EARL OF LAUDERDALE.

MY LORD,                                 Paris, 19 Decembre, 1668.    23131, f. 44.

I have receved from Major Monro the letter your Lo. was plaised
to honnor me with. I dow assour your Lo. all of us in the regiment ar extraimly sensible of your Lo. faveur in this last particu-
laire as we ar also of the formers we have to your Lo.; and I begge
of your Lo. to assour his Majesty that ther is non of his subjects
shall be mor redy to obey his commands nor I and all my regiment,
which we shall allwais dow most faithfully and punctually. My

Lord Major Monro told me that it hes bein reported to your Lo. and to several others that I was maryed hier.   I dow assour your Lo. it is most false, for upon my word of honnor I had nevr any such thothits, and I pray your Lo. to dow that justice to belive that I am incapable to dow a basse actione; and, my Lord, if you hier any such thing spok you will oblige me extraimly to assur the contraire, and to belive I am,

My Lord,

Your Lo. most humbl and most obedient servant,

DOUGLAS.

---

LORD GEORGE DOUGLAS TO THE EARL OF LAUDERDALE.

23131, f. 89.  MY LORD,                                    A Paris, 16 Feb. 1669.

By the last post I gave your Lo. notis of our merche for Vienne en Dauphine, and being destined for Candy, as this will be the absolat rouing and destructione of my regiment, our only resource is to your Lo. to intraite you to spik to the King to spik to the French Ambassadeur, and that his Majesty wold be plaised to wryt hier in our faveurs; for, if my regiment com to be weik, as it will most certinly, we will never be in conditione to mak it up a gaine; and your Lo. knowis that it is all my fortune and my officirs.   As you have alwais bein our frind, now is the only and last strock for to help us.   I have bein with Monsieur de Rouvigny and shoed him how we war not fitt for that service, and how strange it is to send us for our absolut rouing, which he conffessed and hes spok of it to Monsieur de Turenne.   But ther is sum other raisons, for all the holl world admirs why my regiment should be sent.   So, my Lord, our last refuge is to the King and you, that his Majesty wold be plaised to tak our intrests and spik for us serieusly. But what his Majesty dis most be sudenly: and, my Lord, as I wryt to you by my last, I dow not knbw but the Kinges Ambassadeur and the Jnglishe merchants my suffer by it that is in Turky. So, expecting your Lo. speedy ansur, I remaine,

My Lord,

Your Lo. most humbl and most obedient servant,

DOUGLAS.

# INDEX.

www.ingramcontent.com/pod-product-compliance
Lightning Source LLC
Chambersburg PA
CBHW030723110426
42739CB00030B/1360